This Thing Called Breakfast!

Meaning. Signs. Symptoms. Remedies.

Oluwafemi Festus

Table of contents.

Acknowledgement

I wish to say a big thank you to all the amazing and exceptional people in my life who supported in one way or the other to make this book a reality and possibility.

I sincerely appreciate the support I received from Peace, John and Adesuyi who collaborated to proofread and edit this book. Thank you for painstakingly doing this, I love you guys so much!

I also recognize and appreciate the support from Adeyemi who provided ideas towards the mock-ups and graphics design, you are simply the best!

I also appreciate my colleagues, friends and family members who helped in one way or the other towards the publication of this book. I couldn't have asked for a better support system, you guys rock!

My sincere and heartfelt gratitude goes to my heartthrob and baby girl, Oluwatosin. Thank you for the support, commitment and encouragement to finish the piece, I love and appreciate you always!

Introduction.

I have always asked myself this question; is **"Breakfast"** inevitable?

Research and statistics have shown that the rate of heartbreaks, separations and divorce in the world today has been on the increase, especially among this generation.

What is responsible for this high rate of heartbreaks, separation and divorce?

What can be done to reduce this high rate of heartbreaks, separation and divorce?

The truth is that, if you take the issue of breakfast lightly and casually, you might end up being a casualty!

Ecclesiastes 7:12 ''Amplified Bible: For wisdom is a protection even as money is a protection, But the excellent advantage of knowledge is that wisdom shields and preserves the lives of its possessors.''

From the bible reference above, knowledge is not just an advantage, but it will also preserve your life and exempt you from becoming a victim or casualty of life circumstances, such as breakfast!

Like we say in the local parlance here in Nigeria, if you know, you know!
The importance of knowing, that is, having the required and sufficient knowledge about certain issues of life like breakfast cannot be overemphasized.

However, I believe that it is better to be served breakfast before marriage than to ignore the signs and symptoms of breakfast (More information in chapter 3) and go ahead with the relationship which will lead to a failed marriage, separation and ultimately divorce! If proper care is not taken into consideration.

Are you in a relationship at the moment?
Are you planning, thinking or contemplating leaving that relationship?
Or have you just left a relationship due to any reason?
Are you planning to start another relationship anytime soon or in the future?
Regardless of the category you may belong to according to the questions above, the importance of knowledge, especially knowledge about breakfast cannot be ignored or neglected.
As a believer and child of God, you should not be caught in long and immense pains and regrets caused by breakfast.

So, in this book, you will be learning some insider information and revelation on what breakfast is, signs and symptoms of breakfast, relationship between breakfast and betrayal, and remedy /relief from breakfast.

Without a shred of doubt in my mind, I am very confident that this book, with the help of the holy spirit, will give some guides and inspiration to everyone who reads through the tips on how to make decisions to exempt and prevent making mistakes that leads to serving or being served breakfast.

Chapter 1.

[What Is Breakfast?]

In this chapter, we will be talking extensively on what breakfast is all about.

First, it is important that I clarify that the term breakfast used in this book is not a meal eaten in the morning or the first meal of the day.

In normal terms, breakfast is the first meal served in the morning, eaten before noon and usually light weight.

Examples of meals served during breakfast includes : bacon and egg, bread and tea, cereals, milk and waffles, pap and akara or any other simple and light meal.

Dieticians and nutritionists have always emphasized that breakfast is the most important meal of the day and should not be skipped. As the name suggests, breakfast breaks the

overnight fasting period. Breakfast replenishes the supply of glucose to boost your energy levels and alertness, while also providing other essential nutrients required for good health, general living and well-being.
Dieticians and nutritionists further advised that breakfast should not be snacks and junk food, but rather food that contains proteins, minerals, fruits and carbohydrates for energy to fuel your brain, kidneys, heart muscles, and central nervous system.
Those who eat a healthy, nutritious and balanced breakfast have a reduced risk of being exposed to heart diseases, high blood pressure, stroke, diabetes, cardiovascular-related death and other health related issues and diseases.

I must admit that having breakfast is important and should not be ignored if you are not fasting. The only thing that should prevent you from having your breakfast is when you are fasting.
Fasting is when you voluntarily reduce or eliminate your intake of food for a specific time and purpose. Fasting is a spiritual exercise that must be done with the topmost discipline for its effectiveness and result.
Fasting regularly sharpens our spiritual sensitivity, reveals our true spiritual condition, resulting in brokenness, repentance, and a transformed life.
Fasting should not be done without praying. Do not be involved in fasting and omitting or forgetting to pray, that is more like a hunger strike which will not produce any spiritual benefit.

Matthew 17:21 'NKJV Bible: However, this kind does not go out except by prayer and fasting.''

From the bible reference above, for fasting to be effective and to produce the desired result, it must be accompanied by prayers.

Fasting and prayer can also bring about more than just a personal transformation. Fasting and prayer can bring about a revival and a change in the right direction that would ultimately change your destination.

Fasting and prayer can restore and strengthen your intimacy with God. It can also help you to hear God more clearly and accurately. Fasting and prayer helps you to be humble and consecrated to God. Fasting and prayer can also help and build your relationship with the holy spirit.
Aside from all the above spiritual benefits of fasting, fasting also has the following health benefits which includes weight loss by limiting calorie intake and boosting metabolism, decreased blood pressure, reduced inflammation and obesity, boots immune system, helping clear skin and prevention of acne and also helps detox, improves brain function and promotes longevity.
As you can see, fasting is a win-win both spiritually and physically.

Now, the term breakfast used in this book means heartbreak. Breakfast is a word used in Nigeria which means heartbreak or disappointment. Usually expressed as ***"chop breakfast"*** or " ***served breakfast*** ".
On social media and also in local parlance and street here in Nigeria, you may have heard or read, **"Him/She don chop breakfast"** or **"She/He has been served breakfast"**

, it simply means that someone is heartbroken or going through a relationship disappointment.

From my several counselling sessions, I must admit that serving or being served breakfast is not a good experience.

The trauma caused by serving or being served breakfast can be devastating and extremely severe.

No genuine and bona-fide child of God deserves to be served breakfast.

People should learn to avoid heartbreaks, but if you do not get knowledge, especially biblical knowledge, you will end up experiencing heartbreaks and being served several breakfasts!

So many people, including some believers, think that some tasks and activities can exempt them from being served breakfast, funny!

They think that showing off activities like cooking for the man, washing his clothes, giving her money, buying her gifts, going on vacation together, etc can exempt them from a heartbreak, this is very far from the truth!

Trust me, your physical appearance, good fashion sense, and your nice character cannot prevent or exempt you from this thing called breakfast!

Chapter Summary.

In this chapter, we observed that breakfast is not in the context of the first meal of the day, but being referred to

as an activity of a Relationship Breakup. We talked about the importance of breakfast as a meal of the day and the benefits of eating healthy breakfast. We also talked about fasting (which is a Spiritual exercise) and how it should be done to get the maximum result.
Finally, we talked about the meaning of breakfast in the context of this book, which connotes the word heartbreak and relationship disappointment.
In the next chapter, we will be covering the biblical origin of breakfast and some vital lessons.

Chapter 2.

[Biblical Origin]

In the last chapter, we talked extensively about the definition of breakfast and its importance. We further talked about the meaning of the term breakfast used in the context of this book which means to be heartbroken or disappointed in relationships.

In this chapter, we will be talking about the biblical origin of breakfast and some vital lessons to be learned.

Genesis 29:10-30 NKJV
''10 And it came to pass, when Jacob saw Rachel the daughter of Laban his mother's brother, and the sheep

of Laban his mother's brother, that Jacob went near and rolled the stone from the well's mouth, and watered the flock of Laban his mother's brother.
11 Then Jacob kissed Rachel, and lifted up his voice and wept.
12 And Jacob told Rachel that he was her father's relative and that he was Rebekah's son. So she ran and told her father.
13 Then it came to pass, when Laban heard the report about Jacob his sister's son, that he ran to meet him, and embraced him and kissed him, and brought him to his house. So he told Laban all these things.
14 And Laban said to him, "Surely you are my bone and my flesh." And he stayed with him for a month.
15 Then Laban said to Jacob, "Because you are my relative, should you therefore serve me for nothing? Tell me, what should your wages be?"
16 Now Laban had two daughters: the name of the elder was Leah, and the name of the younger was Rachel.
17 Leah's eyes were [a]delicate, but Rachel was beautiful of form and appearance.
18 Now Jacob loved Rachel; so he said, "I will serve you seven years for Rachel your younger daughter."
19 And Laban said, "It is better that I give her to you than that I should give her to another man. Stay with me."
20 So Jacob served seven years for Rachel, and they seemed only a few days to him because of the love he had for her.
21 Then Jacob said to Laban, "Give me my wife, for my days are fulfilled, that I may go in to her."
22 And Laban gathered together all the men of the place and made a feast.

23 Now it came to pass in the evening, that he took Leah his daughter and brought her to Jacob; and he went in to her.
24 And Laban gave his maid Zilpah to his daughter Leah as a maid.
25 So it came to pass in the morning, that behold, it was Leah. And he said to Laban, "What is this you have done to me? Was it not for Rachel that I served you? Why then have you deceived me?"
26 And Laban said, "It must not be done so in our [b]country, to give the younger before the firstborn.
27 Fulfill her week, and we will give you this one also for the service which you will serve with me still another seven years."
28 Then Jacob did so and fulfilled her week. So he gave him his daughter Rachel as wife also.
29 And Laban gave his maid Bilhah to his daughter Rachel as a maid.
30 Then Jacob also went in to Rachel, and he also loved Rachel more than Leah. And he served with Laban still another seven years.''

From the bible reference above, we can see that Jacob was served breakfast i.e he was heartbroken and disappointed when the love of his life Rachel was switched with her elder sister Leah by his Uncle Laban.

Genesis 29:25 '' ***NKJV: So it came to pass in the morning, that behold, it was Leah. And he said to Laban, "What is this you have done to me? Was it not for Rachel that I served you? Why then have you deceived me?"***

From the Bible reference above, we can see the relationship between breakfast and betrayal. If you are heartbroken and disappointed, you will feel betrayed.

Looking closely at the Bible reference Genesis 29: 10-30, we can see some learning points both negative and positive.

The moment Jacob set his eyes on Rachel, he kissed her and wept.

One might think that the action of Jacob kissing and weeping was as a means of him expressing his affection for his Uncle's daughter Rachel, but trust me that was not the case.

Jacob is very smart and cunning. See what he did to impress Rachel before he kissed her.

Genesis 29:10

''MSG:

The moment Jacob spotted Rachel, daughter of Laban his mother's brother, saw her arriving with his uncle Laban's sheep, he went and single-handedly rolled the stone from the mouth of the well and watered the sheep of his uncle Laban.''

After Jacob had displayed to be a superman by single-handedly rolling away the stone, he went ahead to kiss Rachel (Genesis 29:11).

Rachel would not have suspected anything; she might have also been carried away by the physical appearance of Jacob to have allowed him to kiss her. Safe to say, Rachel, let her guards down!

It is not proper to exchange sexual pleasure like kissing the opposite sex when you are not legally married. No matter

the relationship and closeness, there are other ways to exchange pleasantries and show affection besides kissing. This could have been done either by bowing, a handshake or at most a hug and not by kissing.
You might argue it is an innocent kiss, but can you tell what is running in the mind of the person you are kissing? It is better not to put yourself in the middle of sexual temptation.
Well, I have received lots of feedback that giving a peck is better and safer than kissing. I have my reservations about that too. The most important factor here is the state of your heart and your intentions. If your intentions are pure and godly, you can by all means proceed with the peck.
The bible even encourages us to greet one another with warm greetings and in some versions with a holy kiss (1 Corinthians 16:20 and 2 Corinthians 13:12).
However, we must not follow after the manner of unbelievers and trends, whereby peck or kissing is done lustfully.

The next question now should be, why did Jacob kiss Rachel? The simple answer is that he was attracted by Rachel's beauty!
Genesis 29:17 ***''MSG:***
Leah had nice eyes, but Rachel was stunningly beautiful.''
Rachel was not just beautiful, she was fair and stunningly beautiful! Jacob could not hide his feelings, he had to express his feelings for Rachel with a kiss.

Despite this wrong approach to Kissing Rachel, Jacob still did the right thing worth learning.

Genesis 29:18-20 MSG **''18 And it was Rachel that Jacob loved. So Jacob answered, "I will work for you seven years for your younger daughter Rachel."**
19 "It is far better," said Laban, "that I give her to you than marry her to some outsider. Yes. Stay here with me."
20 So Jacob worked seven years for Rachel. But it only seemed like a few days, he loved her so much.''

From the bible reference above, Jacob did not have any pre-marital sex or affair with Rachel, despite the love and affection he had for her.

Jacob properly declared his intentions to Laban and even offered to serve him for seven years, even though they are related by blood.

It is very important to put feelings aside and do what is right and noble. I strongly believe that the guys should learn from this exemplary style of Jacob and inform appropriate parties without sentiments and bias when they begin to develop some form of affection towards a lady.

In addition, Jacob did not elope with Rachel when he was expected to serve for seven years, which eventually became fourteen years, it was all like a few days to him, what a strong love and affection he had for Rachel!

The Love between Jacob and Rachel was backed up by a strong commitment.

Sisters, if the brother claims to love you and he is not willing to show any sign of responsibility and commitment, I advise you to be careful and not make any decision to accept their proposals.

I have been privileged to advise several young people in relationships and I have always maintained the stand that while you are friends, you should be open and when you begin a romantic relationship with marriage in view, you must be committed.

Commitment is not what you give to someone you do not intend to spend your future and the rest of your life with!

Commitment is a sign of true love. You cannot claim to love someone and not be willing to commit. Moreover, you don't only declare your commitment in relationships, you show and demonstrate commitment as well.

Jacob was not only open to expressing his love to Rachel; he was also committed to marrying her. To be open minded in your relationship is good, but to be committed is even much better!

If your relationship has not grown from openness/transparency to commitment, breakfast is inevitable!

You cannot claim to be committed to what you are not willing to sacrifice for. There is no measure of sacrifice one cannot give when there is commitment. Commitment is not a competition, but it should be mutual.

Commitment is not something you plead or beg for, commitment is something that comes naturally from the place of proper and genuine love. If your partner is struggling to show it, and not just saying he or she is committed to you, the relationship is already questionable and breakfast might be inevitable!

Brothers, take a cue from Jacob and show true love backed by commitment and responsibility to that Sister! Never

proceed to propose to someone you are not willing and able to be committed to, it is a sure recipe for breakfast and ultimately a failed marriage that will be endured and not enjoyed!
Sisters, take a cue from Rachel, do not be disobedient to your parents, either biological or spiritual. Rachel, out of love could have convinced Jacob otherwise not to follow the due process to finalize the marriage rights. If Rachel had put pressure on Jacob, he might have compromised and even engage in a premarital affair.

Chapter Summary.

In this chapter, we observed the biblical origin of breakfast and some invaluable lessons. We learned about the place of commitment in validating the genuineness of a relationship, especially with the opposite sex.

In the next chapter, we will be covering the signs and symptoms of breakfast.

Chapter 3.

[Signs and Symptoms]

In the last chapter, we talked about the biblical origin of breakfast. We observed critically, the exemplary love life between Jacob and Rachel and some invaluable lessons that are still relevant to date.

In this chapter, we will be talking about the signs and symptoms of breakfast to look out for.

Signs are objective, observable factors that can be identified by another person. Signs are yet to occur in events or situations, but it is a signal that it might occur if no correction is made.

Symptoms are subjective experiences that can only be identified by anyone going through an experience. Symptoms are current happenings, but the effect and consequence of what is happening may still be unknown or unclear to the one going through it. Symptoms may not even be your experience; they can also be your feelings.

I am a firm believer in the statement that prevention is better than cure, and I prefer to be on the offensive, rather than to be on the defensive.

Proverbs 27:12 NLT

''A prudent person foresees danger and takes precautions. The simpleton goes blindly on and suffers the consequences."

From the bible reference above, we can see the importance of not ignoring pointers, red-flags, signs and symptoms of anything, especially breakfast since it relates to the heart.

I strongly advise that you pay rapt attention to this chapter. The consequence of ignoring signs and symptoms can be very devastating, extremely severe and maybe irrecoverable due to the fragility of the heart.

My prayer for you is that the Holy Spirit will open your ears, eyes and heart to receive and understand these signs and symptoms.

For ease of understanding, I will categorize these signs and symptoms into key areas in the relationship, and they include spiritual, physical, emotional and financial.

SPIRITUAL SIGNS AND SYMPTOMS

The spiritual signs and symptoms are the most important aspect to look out for. However, it is the most overlooked.

People are busy looking for physical, emotional, and financial signs and symptoms while ignoring the spiritual signs and symptoms.

I am not against looking out for physical, emotional and financial signs and symptoms, but the utmost priority should be given to these spiritual signs and symptoms. If you ignore spiritual signs and symptoms, it is sure that one must be served breakfast, and if you decide to proceed with the marriage, instead of enjoying the marriage, you will end up enduring the marriage. Do not say God forbid, rather you should give more priority to these spiritual signs and symptoms.

Trust me, the spiritual controls the physical, emotional and financial.

It is very unfortunate that our society nowadays even discourages people from paying attention to spiritual signs and symptoms.

I want to plead with you not to join the multitude to ignore the spiritual signs and symptoms in a relationship, it is not the multitude that will endure and go through the unpleasant and devastating severe consequences that will result at the end, it is you!

That being said, let us look at some of these spiritual signs and symptoms.

2 Corinthians 6:14 Amplified Bible

‘’Do not be unequally bound together with unbelievers [do not make mismatched alliances with them, inconsistent with your faith]. For what partnership can righteousness have with lawlessness? Or what fellowship can light have with darkness?"

From the bible reference above, the first spiritual sign to look out for and consider is the **Faith of your partner** .

The Faith of your partner is not determined by their names or even the religion of your partner. This is not also determined by being a churchgoer. Anyone can go to church!

I know a certain Paul Pogba, he is a popular footballer, going by the first name of Paul, you would think he is a Christian, but he is a Muslim. I used to be Oluwafemi Kareem and a lot of people thought I was a Muslim, but I was not. Well, I have successfully changed my name officially to Oluwafemi Festus.

How do you confirm the Faith of your partner?

You can confirm their Faith through their beliefs, philosophies about life, ideologies and convictions.

If your partner's beliefs and convictions differ extremely from yours, you should have it at the back of your mind that breakfast might just happen to you and even become inevitable.

The next spiritual sign to look out for is the presence of the fear of God in your partner. It is extremely important that you do not just share the same faith with your partner, but your partner must have the fear of God.

If your partner does not have the fear of God, even though they share the same faith with you, it will be easier for them to lie, cheat and even beat you! It is extremely important that your partner does not just love God, but that he or she fears God too!

The last spiritual sign you should look out for and consider is the presence of the fruits of the Holy Spirit.

Now that you have confirmed you both share the same faith, that is still not enough, you must also consider how many fruit(s) of the Holy Spirit your partner has.

Galatians 5:22-23 NLT

‘’22: But the Holy Spirit produces this kind of fruit in our lives: love, joy, peace, patience, kindness, goodness, faithfulness,

23: gentleness, and self-control. There is no law against these things!"

From the bible reference above, we can see that there are Nine (9) fruits of the Holy Spirit. These fruits are so important and should not be ignored. I remembered asking my partner how many fruits of the Holy Spirit she has, she was honest enough not to mention all Nine (9) of them.

She has more than five (5) of these fruits and I am satisfied! I am encouraging her to grow because she can achieve all Nine (9) of them.

Have it at the back of your mind that It is not about mentioning how many fruits of the spirit you have, it must be seen, noticeable and evident in your life.

Mathew 7:16 NLT

''You can identify them by their fruit, that is, by the way they act. Can you pick grapes from thornbushes, or figs from thistles?''

The bible reference above corroborates the importance of paying attention to spiritual signs through fruits of the Holy Spirit.

It is extremely important to know that you cannot exude the fruits of the Holy Spirit if you do not have the Holy Spirit in you. The Holy Spirit only dwells in a saved, Holy, clean and consecrated vessel.

If your partner has none or just One (1) fruit of the Holy Spirit, it is a red-flag that should not be ignored.

In summary, your partner should have the same faith as you, fear God and have fruits of the spirit.

PHYSICAL SIGNS AND SYMPTOMS

The next category we will be observing is the physical signs and symptoms. As much as the spiritual signs are very important, the physical signs should not be ignored or overlooked.

So many spirit-filled people are struggling in their relationships and marriages because they ignored these physical signs and symptoms. Having the fruits of the

Holy Spirit does not mean that you should ignore physical signs, else breakfast will be served!
The physical signs are what you can see and touch or what touches you. They are something tangible and real.
One of these physical signs includes your look. If your partner is always complaining about your looks or appearance, do not ignore it. It might mean you are not up to their standards when it comes to physical appearance. It might be excessive make-up, absurd fashion etc
The truth is, there is always room for improvement and your partner should give compliments about your physical looks and not complaints. It gets worse when your partner only criticizes, compares and condemns your physical looks. Do not ignore or overlook this sign!
In addition, another physical sign you should not ignore is physical abuse in whatever form. Never overlook this physical sign. Physical abuse can also come as domestic violence to people around the person you are in a relationship with and this should not be ignored or overlooked. That He or She is beating or abusing people around should be enough sign that you might be next in the line!
Furthermore, domestic affairs such as cleaning the house, cooking etc is a physical sign you should not ignore. This is a responsibility both parties should be willing to get themselves involved In. Well, we can say that this mentioned activity is primarily the responsibility of the woman, but the man should be willing to assist when the need arises. Physical signs are worth talking about and should not be overlooked as it is capable of leading to breakfast being served!

FINANCIAL SIGNS AND SYMPTOMS

Another category of signs and symptoms we are observing and that should not be overlooked is that relating to financial matters. Financial and money matters should not be ignored, ignore them at your risk!

If your partner is stingy or selfish, this is a direct entry to breakfast! There is a difference between being prudent and being stingy or selfish. True love gives! Now, money is not the only thing you can give in a relationship, you can give your time, knowledge and any other thing that is required to make the relationship blossom.

Another sign under this category is not revealing your financial worth. I have received feedback that if your partner knows your net worth, he or she might have excessive demands from you. This is far from the truth because a spirit-filled partner will not take advantage of the information to exploit you. If you cannot trust your partner with your financial worth, then the relationship is not worth it.

True love is not just demonstrated through commitment, but also through openness and transparency.

Finally, another sign here is giving gifts randomly, especially during celebrations. If your partner does not recognize and appreciate you with gift(s), it is a red-flag. Your partner might be ignorant of this, but you can mention it and have a discussion around it. Their response should help you unravel if the forgetfulness is willingly or out of ignorance.

It is worthy to note that if your partner is always and only after your money, this is a major red-flag and a sign that should not be ignored. There must be modesty. Do not allow anyone to put you under unnecessary pressure to satisfy their financial appetite. This is also not a license to laziness or nonchalance. You should be worried if your partner is not accepting your financial assistance, even if he or she has more than enough, love will compel you to give and love will also compel you to receive.

EMOTIONAL SIGNS AND SYMPTOMS

Without an iota of doubt, this is arguably a controversial sign and symptom you should never ignore. Aside from the spiritual signs and symptoms which are the most important, emotional signs and symptoms follow afterward.

What differentiates the physical from emotional signs and symptoms is that while the first can be seen, touched, and heard, the latter can be felt and the effects are more severe. Emotional signs and symptoms are very subtle and may not be easily noticed until the deed and damage has been done.

The first emotional sign you should not ignore is the lack of communication. Effective communication is not really in the length, quantity and duration, rather it is the thought, consistency and feedback.

How can you not talk to your lover for more than 24 hours? How??

I need to address this ideology of waiting for the other to put a call first. Who initiates the first phone call at the dawn of the day or last call at the end of the day does not matter! You should only be worried if you put a call across and there was no feedback or response. However,

communication must be mutual! We need to discard the mentality that the call must always come from one person, so if he doesn't call, Sister, please call to check up on him. If she doesn't call, Brother, please call to check up on her!
You should be extremely worried when your partner can go the whole day without communicating with you. I said communicate and not just talk. Talking is not the only form of communication, even though there are other forms of communication such as texting, chatting via Social media, letters, etc. If your partner begins to find it extremely difficult to communicate with you, then breakfast is inevitable!
Another emotional sign you should never ignore is not paying or receiving attention from your partner. The moment you are unable to get the attention of your partner, breakfast is probably cooking and about to be served hot. You only pay attention to what is on your priority list.
Do not allow work or any other task or activities take all your priority and cause you to ignore or neglect your partner. You must also learn to communicate and show your partner that they matter and will always have your attention.

Furthermore, another emotional sign is lack and loss of mutual respect. It is funny how your partner disrespects you in a relationship and you do not see it as a big deal. Although respect is a big deal and an ice breaker for the guys, the ladies also need to be respected. The respect being discussed is not that of kneeling or calling by titles eg 'Sir'. Respect is in value and attitude to which you relate with your partner. You only respect what you value!

Do not allow anyone to treat you like they are doing you a favor for being in a relationship with you! You are a spec that deserves nothing but the best! Trust me, if there is a lack of mutual respect, it is only a matter of when and not if breakfast will be served or not!

Finally, trust is an emotional sign you should never ignore! If your partner does not trust you anymore or wants you to prove your trust at all times, this is a major red-flag. If your partner is always insecure whenever you are talking with other people, especially the opposite sex, then trust is lacking and it is only a matter of time before breakfast is served hot!
I agree that there should be an element of jealousy from your partner, but not the extent of producing lack of trust and insecurities.

The following are list of other emotional sign you should pay attention to;
1. You only feel annoyed by each other.
2. The proximity of the other person makes you feel uncomfortable and maybe irritated.
3. You no longer tolerate each other. All you see is fault, error and mistakes.
4. You can imagine a life without your partner and you are already thinking or looking for someone else.
5. You no longer support, encourage and motivate each other.
6. You have different ideas, visions and philosophies about the future.

7. You no longer make an effort to be attractive to each other.
8. Your relationship burdens you more than it brings you joy. There is even an absence of peace of mind.
9. You are thinking about separation and space and not closure or closeness.
10. One takes advantage of the other without any remorse.

Chapter Summary.

In this chapter, we talked about the signs and symptoms of breakfast that we should not ignore.
We categorized the signs and symptoms into Four (4) major parts which includes spiritual, physical, emotional and emotional.

In the next chapter, we will be talking about solutions i.e. relief and remedies to breakfast.

Chapter 4.

[Remedy and Relief]

In the last chapter, we talked about the signs and symptoms of breakfast to look out for and take necessary precautions against. We categorized these signs into spiritual, physical, financial and emotional.

I emphasized that the spiritual should be the priority, followed by emotional and then physical and financial.

In this chapter, we will be talking about the remedies and reliefs to victims of breakfast. This chapter seeks to provide succor and solution that helps heal from the effects of the consequences of being served or serving breakfast.

Have you been served breakfast recently? Are you hurting, angry, confused, crying or even sick?

I have a piece of good news for you! There are remedies and relief that will provide healing for your broken heart. Your heart can be mended if only you can commit to mending it the right way.

Most people after being served breakfast and going through heartbreak, they are immediately on the lookout to start another relationship to prove a point that they are fine. What they fail to realize is that the hurt and anger they felt from their past relationship will be transferred and expressed in the new relationship if not treated properly. It is only a matter of time before the pain and anger of the breakfast will resurface.

I must admit that breakfast can be devastating and it is capable of leading one to depression and in worse case, suicide.

It is important to know that before you seek a solution to a relationship heartbreak, you must understand what led to the breakfast. Do not take any act in ignorance, it only recycles the pain!

There is a great need to evaluate and assess yourself to discover what led to the heartbreak. This is not the time to blame yourself or anyone. You need to fight the temptation of blaming and condemning yourself or anyone.

It is good and okay to express your feeling of heartbreak, maybe by crying or being sober, but you do not have to dwell on it for long and you do not have to hurt and inflict much pain on yourself.

Getting relief and remedy from heartbreak is not a quick fix, it takes time. Heartbreak or breakfast is actually like a wound or injury that affects your heart and healing is not instant, it takes processes. Healing and total recovery from a heartbreak is not what you conclude within a day or two, it could take days, months or even years. You can move on within a day or two but the healing and mending of the heart that has been broken takes time and you must allow time to run its course to perfect the healing, else the wound or injury to your heart will be reopened. But there are things you can do to support yourself through the healing process and protect your emotional wellbeing.

First, before you begin the journey to your recovery and the mending of your heart, you must decide that there is no going back. It gets worse when you are undecided. Indecision is a decision itself, only that it leads to more problems and complications. Make a promise to yourself that there is no going back! You must be firm and assertive with your decision and your mind must be made up that there is no going or turning back. There will be several pleas, persuasion and even advice from people you respect and hold in high esteem to go back, never go back to an abusive relationship; be it physical abuse or emotional abuse, never go back!

I want you to believe me that there are proven remedies and relief from heartbreak. The end of a relationship should not be the end of your dreams, destiny and life. I assure you by the integrity and faithfulness of God, you can heal and recover from any form of heartbreak.

The following tips will help you heal and recover from breakfast.

1. ACKNOWLEDGE AND GRIEVE IF NEED BE.

The first remedy and relief from breakfast are to acknowledge that you are hurting. You are free to grieve and cry in the process of acknowledgment, but do not dwell in that grieve. You are no less a man or woman when you acknowledge and admit that you are hurting. Stop forming that hard girl that you are not or hard guy, and do not believe that you will be perceived to be weak when you admit you are hurting. Permit yourself to feel and express all the sadness, anger, loneliness, and other emotions that come with heartbreak.

Do not ignore or deny the outcomes that the breakfast is having on you, because self-deception is the worst type of deception and no remedy or relief will be achieved via that route.

Do not mistake acknowledgment for acceptance. What I am trying to say is that, do not acknowledge heartbreak and accept or believe that there are no remedy or relief to breakfast.

2. TALK TO SOMEONE YOU TRUST.

The next remedy and relief from heartbreak are to talk to someone you trust. In your quest to talk, don't just talk to anyone, talk to someone you know and trust. Talking to just anyone might lead to the person gossiping about you. You can talk to a close friend or best friend who will not mock you and make jest of you. You can also talk to your Parents or guardian. You can also talk to your Pastor or a spiritual authority over you. You can also talk to a professional psychologist or certified relationship and marriage counselor.

It is better to talk to someone who has the experience to guide you than to talk to someone who does not have any experience in what you are going through. However, if you cannot find someone you trust with the required experience, you can talk to someone you trust that is highly knowledgeable, caring, and interested in your well-being not just physically but more importantly spiritually and emotionally.

It is important to know that it is not good to keep silent or keep to yourself after experiencing this thing called breakfast, it can lead to depression and even suicide if not urgently resolved. There is a popular saying that a problem shared is a problem half solved. Permit me to say a breakfast story shared is a heartbreak half mended or solved. However, you have to be mindful and exercise caution not to speak to just anyone.

3. SET HEALTHY BOUNDARIES.

Another remedy from breakfast is to set healthy boundaries between you and your ex, either the one you served breakfast or that served you breakfast or that from unforeseen circumstances such as difference in genotype, lack of parental consent etc. Setting boundaries does not mean that you both should not exchange pleasantries to each other or say hello once in a while again, it means reducing the rate of communication or putting measures in place to avoid close contacts. Setting boundaries will help you maintain your sanity and improve your emotional stability.

Do not be aggressive and extreme in setting boundaries whereby you delete contacts, report and black blackmail your ex, etc. rather set boundaries that would maintain a cordial relationship in a platonic way, but avoid close contacts of any sort.

Setting healthy boundaries may include the following;

* The avoidance of midnight and long phone conversations,
* Avoid surprises and giving or accepting gifts.
* Avoid frequent personal hangouts etc.

4. AVOID IDLENESS.

To further heal from heartbreak, you must avoid idleness. There is a popular saying that an idle mind is the devil's workshop. Trust me, so many immoral, ungodly and carnal thoughts will fill your mind when you are idle, especially after you have served or have been served breakfast. The devil will begin to manipulate and control your mind because you are idle. Going through heartbreak is not an excuse to stop going to work, going to church, or attending seminars, events, and masterclasses or pursuing your life career.

The truth is that you will get over heartbreak faster when you are engaged than when you are idle. Idleness can lead to deep thinking, depression, and ultimately suicide.

You must fight idleness by not hiding yourself. Take yourself out for a treat, go see a movie, read a book and do what makes you happy at the moment.

I strongly advise that you use the time at your disposal to be engaged in something meaningful and productive that would be beneficial to your life. Just ensure you are adding value and making an impact!

Avoiding idleness will make you meet and network with people, make new friends, etc. and who knows, you might even meet the one who will love you genuinely!

5. FILL THE VACUUM.

Further to the advice above to avoid idleness, there is still an emptiness inside you that just any activity or events cannot fill. There is a space, vacuum and emptiness that

can only be filled by God. No other activity, events or even any man or woman can fill this vacuum.
So many people, including believers, have ignorantly tried to use food, parties, events, new relationships, and worse still premarital sex to fill this emptiness, only to discover that they are still empty, unsatisfied, and unfulfilled.
Man, (either male or female) is a spirit being that lives in the body. Priority must be given to the spirit through the soul which is also known as the mind and not the body. Filling the vacuum in the body and ignoring the spirit will still result in heartaches.
Now, how do you fill this vacuum in your spirit? The remedy to filling this vacuum is to get the living word of God inside by reading, studying and meditating on the word of God daily.
A daily dose of the word of God is the real deal as it provides Contentment, Joy, Love, and peace. Devotionals can be of great help to studying the word of God and you can get a bible plan that helps you study the word of God effectively. You must be disciplined, determined and dedicated to fill this emptiness in your spirit.
Once you fill the emptiness in your spirit, it is only a matter of time before all other vacuums on the outside will be filled.

6. OPEN YOUR HEART TO LOVE AGAIN.

As the healing and mending of your heart are almost concluded, you must open your heart to love again. First, open your heart and accept the love from God, and next the love from friends and family around you, and lastly, the love from a faithful partner.

Do not allow the bitter experience of breakfast cause you to shut your heart permanently to love. Do not join the multitude to generalize the popular saying that "men are scum or that women are gold diggers". Love is indeed a beautiful thing.

However, you must go through the first 5 tips before you open your heart again to love. If you open your heart to love immediately after breakfast, you will only expand on the wound and not mend it.

7. BE GRATEFUL AND LEARN FROM THE BREAKFAST EXPERIENCE.

The last tip is to be grateful and learn from the breakfast experience. Be grateful first to God that you are alive and for the strength and grace to go through the hurt of heartbreak without breaking.

Next is to be grateful to the wonderful people God has placed around you who stood by you, encouraged, and helped you in one way or another during the breakfast experience. Not everyone who went through the breakfast experience survived it. So many people have been emotionally destabilized and mentally deranged since an experience of a breakfast was served, and unable to recover.

Lastly, you must ensure you learn from the breakfast experience, else you might be a victim again.

I find it disturbing that some people have been served breakfast several times and I wonder if they ever learned from their previous breakfast experience because the story of what led to the first breakfast will be similar. I asked myself, is it that they do not value their wellbeing?
I believe that now that you know better, you will do better!
Never ignore or trivialize the lessons from your breakfast experience or that of those close to you, if you ignore the lessons, you will suffer the consequences!

Now that you have learned these tips, you should practice them when the need arises and you will see the result, which is the healing to your heart.
I strongly believe that these tips will help mend your broken heart and heal any heartbreak you may have experienced or currently experiencing.
You might need to get an accountability partner that you can share reports with and also get feedback on how you are doing. If you don't have anyone, you can send me an email, I will be glad to assist.

Chapter Summary.

In this chapter, we learned that there are remedies and reliefs for breakfast. Breakfast might lead to heartbreak, but that should not be the end of your life. There are principles, keys and tips that can help you recover from breakfast and make you stronger, wiser and even smarter.

In the next chapter, we will be talking about the possibility of a life without breakfast.

Chapter 5.

[A Life Without Breakfast]

In the last chapter, we talked about remedies and relief from any form of heartbreak. I will advise you to give attention to the chapter even if you have not been served breakfast. You can use the information and knowledge from the chapter to encourage and teach those around you going through heartbreaks.

In this chapter, we will be talking about the possibility of a life without breakfast.
This chapter seeks to answer the question; **is it possible to live a life void of the breakfast show?**
The short and simple answer is Yes!
I am amazed at the wrong notion that is trending, especially on social media that you cannot go through a lifetime without breakfast.
That everyone you know or around you is going through a form of breakfast, does not imply or mean that you too will also go through a breakfast show. The information, knowledge and secret in this chapter will exempt you from breakfast!

The secret to living a life without breakfast is the level and your extent of your love for God! If you love God passionately i.e. with all your heart, soul, mind and body, I assure you that you will never be served breakfast!
I find it extremely disturbing and worrisome that teenagers and even some youth are crazy about starting a romantic relationship with the opposite sex without first having a firm and sound love relationship with their maker, God.
Trust me, to be in a God-centre romantic relationship in some years to come, you must first find your fulfillment in Christ by expressing your love to God. Do not just say or sing that you love God, you must show it!
Therefore, how do you show or measure that you truly love God?

John 14:15 Amplified Bible

''If you [really] love Me, you will keep and obey My commandments.''

From the bible reference above, Jesus said the true measure of your love for Him is by the degree and extent that you keep and obey all of His commandments and instructions. The instructions and commandment of God can be found in the scriptures and you must be ready and willing to obey all and not some of it.

The stronger your faith and love for God, the better you will be able to love another person! The best place to find true love is in the house of God. However, you must be careful and have a discerning spirit from God as there are now so many pretenders and prey, even in the house of God.

In case you do not know, let me tell you that until you have a relationship with God that is above everything and anyone else, you will likely have someone who is more important to you than God and breakfast will become inevitable!

God should not and must not be your last resort! You must learn to intentionally put God in front, you might be scorned and get feedback like you are too old school, just ignore the naysayers and focus on loving God passionately and serving Him.

It is extremely vital and important that God comes first in your life, and the good news is that God is always available and accessible, His arms are always wide open to receive you no matter how far you have derailed from His path.

Trust me, no one and no friend, male or female can always be there for you like God can. He needs to be the one you run to when you are lonely, bored, sad, etc.

No one including your friends, family, parents and even pastor is meant to take the place of God in our lives and heart.

Matthew 22:37-38 NKJV
" 37: Jesus said to him, "'You shall love the LORD your God with all your heart, with all your soul, and with all your mind.'
38: This is the first and great commandment.''

From the bible reference above, we can see that loving God with all our heart, soul and mind is not even advice, it is a command and we must comply with it every day of our lifetime.
Do not be in a rush to enter a romantic relationship, rather take your time to love God first, all that love, affection and attention, and commitment you want to give to that Brother or Sister, give them all to God!
Stop chasing after that Sister or Brother, when you love God, He has a way of connecting you two together.
If you are already in a relationship and you do not love God, it is only a matter of when and not if you will be served breakfast. I encourage you to give priority to loving God passionately and showing it too by being actively involved in serving God and doing His work here on earth.
I want you to know that God loves you more than you can think or imagine. He will never leave you nor forsake you!
Stop looking for someone to love you, you are already loved and chosen by God!

Chapter Summary.

In this chapter, we learned about the possibility of living a life without breakfast i.e. heartbreak. The secret to this type and kind of life is loving God passionately. You cannot love God wholeheartedly and still be heartbroken, it is impossible!

Wrapping Up.

You have been on quite a journey in the last few pages of this book.

I truly hope and believe that you have learned something that will help mend and heal your broken heart.

We have learned about the meaning of the word 'breakfast'. You are no longer in ignorance of the word anymore. We have also talked about the different types and kinds of breakfast.

More importantly, we learned that breakfast is not a respecter of gender, class, education level, financial stability, physical appearance etc. Safe to say, anyone can be served breakfast!

We also went back in memory lane to the biblical origin of breakfast and vital lessons that can help us now to recognize and overcome heartbreak.

In addition, we talked extensively about the signs and symptoms of breakfast. The truth is that if you take the signs lightly and casually, you might end up as a casualty of the effect and dangers of breakfast! The signs are red flags that should not be ignored for anything. I believe it is better to see the sign and take action than ignore them and suffer for it.

Just as signs and symptoms might not be enough, we also talked about remedy and relief for victims of breakfast who might have ignored or overlooked the subtle signs before heartbreak. It is good to know that heartbreak is not the end of your destiny. Although the scars may be there, you will still triumph. It is better to fall and stand than to remain on the floor of defeat due to heartbreak from breakfast.

This book will never be complete without arming you with the information, knowledge and secret that you can live a life without breakfast! In the last chapter, we talked extensively and comprehensively about how to be exempted from breakfast and this can only be achieved

when we love God first with all and not part of our heart, soul and mind.
Loving God first must be our priority if we must be exempted from breakfast.

There is no pleasant breakfast experience, you will hear some experiences and be moved to tears.
Ignorance is part of the reason for breakfast, you must fight ignorance intentionally with knowledge from the word of God and those who have gone ahead of you.
I want to encourage you to buy and share this book with as many as possible that you know might be going through the breakfast experience, you never know, you might be saving a life and preserving a generation!
Even if you do not know or have anyone going through breakfast, you can share this book with teenagers and youths that are still single and not in a romantic relationship, the information and knowledge in this book will be extremely helpful and a guide in making destiny decisions.
As I round off, if you need someone to talk to or pray with you as you go through your breakfast experience, I will be more than glad to hear or read from you. I reply to all my chats and email, so you can be assured that you will not be ignored.
You will surely testify!

Thank you so much for taking your time to read and share with others to buy, God bless you!

ABOUT THE AUTHOR

Oluwafemi Festus aka Bishop, Global Bishop and Global Vision is passionate about God and godliness.

He is a student and teacher of the word of God, motivational speaker, financial advisor, blogger and author of several successful digital books.

He is an entrepreneur and founder of Bishop Concepts and Services, a start-up that deals with creation, implementation and transformation of ideas to value that guarantees results! You can engage His services at https://bishopconcepts.com.ng

Oluwafemi also Co-hosts the podcast titled, MORE (Moment of Refreshing) with Oluwatosin Dorcas on https://anchor.fm/moretalknaija

Oluwafemi' s mission is to excellently educate, empower, enable, encourage and entertain everyone he encounters by ensuring Jesus is revealed and glorified!

Oluwafemi is an addicted lover of God and a strong advocate against premarital sex and sexual immorality, especially among teenagers, youth, and young adults.

He is available on the following social media platforms with the handles below;

Twitter: https://twitter.com/GlobalOluwafemi

Instagram:
https://www.instagram.com/oluwafemi_festus/

Facebook: https://www.facebook.com/bishop.o.festus/

LinkedIn:
https://www.linkedin.com/in/koluwafemifestus/

WhatsApp: https://wa.link/q4gwys

Email: koluwafemifestus@gmail.com

www.ingramcontent.com/pod-product-compliance
Lightning Source LLC
LaVergne TN
LVHW020528160826
845677LV00015B/3965

* 9 7 9 8 8 4 4 4 4 7 7 1 6 *